Dileep Keshava Narayana

Network & Internet Technology & Design

Dileep Keshava Narayana

Network & Internet Technology & Design

LAP LAMBERT Academic Publishing

Imprint
Any brand names and product names mentioned in this book are subject to trademark, brand or patent protection and are trademarks or registered trademarks of their respective holders. The use of brand names, product names, common names, trade names, product descriptions etc. even without a particular marking in this work is in no way to be construed to mean that such names may be regarded as unrestricted in respect of trademark and brand protection legislation and could thus be used by anyone.

Cover image: www.ingimage.com

Publisher:
LAP LAMBERT Academic Publishing
is a trademark of
International Book Market Service Ltd., member of OmniScriptum Publishing Group
17 Meldrum Street, Beau Bassin 71504, Mauritius

Printed at: see last page
ISBN: 978-613-9-90799-1

Zugl. / Approved by: London, University of Greenwich, Network & Internet Technology Design - Coursework, 2012

Table of Contents :

Dileep Keshava Narayana
dileep007k@gmail.com

1. Objective

The objective of this coursework is to create a client/server model communication over an IP network, simulate it and investigate the applications and devices performance.

2. Overview

OPNET provides a virtual network environment which can used to prepare the network model virtually before implementing the network in real time. We can observe the behaviour of the entire network including the components such as server, hubs, switches, routers, applications, and protocols. OPNET helps the individuals such as IT managers, system planners to implement the real model virtually and it also helps network administrators, system administrators, Network engineers to diagnose the problems in the network effectively. OPNET also helps to diagnose the performance and to plan whether the existing model supports expansion of network or not.

In this coursework, step by step explanation of designing a client server network model for WHSB organization whose Headquarters office is located in London, UK. It will consists of 2 branches mainly in Atlanta, US and Tokyo, Japan which gathers and distributes monthly, annual reports of sales handled by the headquarters office London, UK.

1. In scenario 1, Atlanta will consist of 30 users connected to 100 base T switch. Tokyo consists of 25 users connected to 10 base T switch. Both branches will provide the applications such as local printer, email (heavy), web browsing (heavy – http) and FTP (light). Web browsing (Heavy - http) and FTP (light) are supported remotely in both branches. Printer and database (light) are local in Atlanta. Database (Heavy) is locally provided by Tokyo. Atlanta and Tokyo will consist of 10 users running online video conferencing application.

2. In scenario 2, Atlanta will consist of 20 users and 10 users separately connected to hub; hub will be connected to 100 base T switch. Tokyo will consist of 15 users and 10 users separately connected to hub; hub will be connected to 10 base T switch. Both branches will provide the applications such as local printer, email (heavy), web browsing (heavy – http) and FTP (light). Web browsing (Heavy - http) and FTP (light) are supported remotely in both branches. Printer and database (light) are local in Atlanta. Database (Heavy) is locally provided by Tokyo. Atlanta and Tokyo will consist of 10 users running online video conferencing application.

3. Next, we will simulate the created network models above and investigate the results obtained from the utilization of T1 link, average FTP download response time, HTTP page response time (Seconds), behaviour of voice and video conference application, and Ethernet delay.

1

4. At the end, we will expand the network by creating new local office in Osaka, Japan for both 1 & 2 models, and investigate the behaviour of video conferencing application.

3. Building a Network model

3.1 Scenario 1

3.1.1 Create a new project

To create a new project

1. Start OPNET modeler 16.1 from start menu > All programs > Networking > OPNET Modeler.

2. Choose new from the File menu.

3. Select Project and click OK.

4. Name the Project as Cwf and scenario as cs1.

5. Once you get the Start-up wizard: Initial topology select Create empty scenario, and click Next.

6. Next in Startup wizard: Choose Network Scale select Choose from maps and click on Next.

7. Next in Startup wizard: Choose Map add to selected (background first) uk_regions, usa and japan.

8. Next in Startup wizard: Select technologies click include yes for client_Server, Ethernet_advanced and click Finish.

3.1.2 Create Subnets at London, Atlanta and Tokyo in map

1. To create subnet in London, zoom to London first in map and then click on object palette, select subnet and drag to London.

2. To create subnet in Atlanta, zoom to Atlanta in map and then click on object palette, select subnet and drag to Atlanta.

3. To create subnet in Tokyo, zoom to Tokyo in map and then click on object palette, select subnet and drag to Tokyo.

2

3.1.3 Name the subnets

1. Right click on the subnet at London and click set name. Set name as WHSB_London_UK_HQ and click OK.

2. Right click on the subnet at Atlanta and click set name. Set name as WHSB_Atlanta_US and click OK.

3. Right click on the subnet at Tokyo and click set name. Set name as WHSB_Tokyo_Japan and click OK.

3.1.4 WHSB_London_UK_HQ Subnet

1. Double-click on the WHSB_HQ subnet, Select View >Background > Set properties and Set units to Meters. Uncheck checkbox for Satellite orbits.

2. AS_GRF1600_16S_A4_AE24_F12_SLI6 router meets our demands for creating this network model.

We will make use of Ethernet_sli8_gtwy_adv as a firewall to protect the data in the headquarters and to stop external access of the data.

We will step up and configure VPN so that other branch offices in WHSB_Atlanta_US and WHSB_Tokyo_Japan can access Web browsing and FTP services remotely and securely. If the VPN is not configured properly the services like database (Heavy), webbrowsing, FTP and the like services might be blocked by the firewall.

3. Open object palette by clicking on the object palette button from toolbar.

4. Right click on AS_GRF1600_16S_A4_AE24_F12_SLI6 router and click on add to default palette.

5. Drag and Place one AS_GRF1600_16S_A4_AE24_F12_SLI6 router, one ethernet_slip8_gtwy_adv, one ip32_cloud, one ip vpn config, and five Ethernet_server_adv from object palette.

3

6. Rename   AS_GRF1600_16S_AE24_F12_SLI6   router,   ethernet_slip8_gtwy_adv, ip32_cloud, ip vpn config, and five ethernet_server_adv as HQ_Router, HQ_Firewall, HQ_Internet,   VPN_Config,   and   Web_Server_HQ,   Database_Server_HQ, FTP_Server_HQ, Email_Server_HQ, Conference_Server_HQ respectively.

7. Connect   Web_Server_HQ,   Database_Server_HQ,   FTP_Server_HQ, Email_Server_HQ, Conference_Server_HQ to HQ_Router by using 100baseT_adv link from object palette.

8. Connect HQ_Router to HQ_Firewall with T1 link from the object palette.

9. Connect HQ_Router to HQ_Internet with T1 link from the object palette.

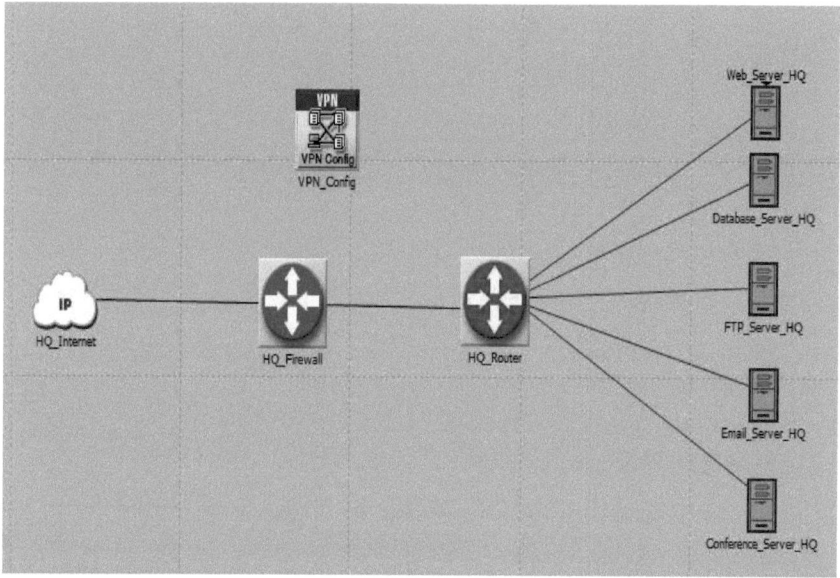

3.1.5 VPN configuration

We must configure VPN otherwise services like file transfer and video conferencing might not work.

To configure VPN, right click on VPN_Config and click on edit attributes.

1. Click on VPN configuration > edit.

2. Click on rows select as 2.

4

3. Click on the row 1 tunnel source name edit type as Atlanta_Router and then click on tunnel destination name edit type as HQ_Router.

4. Make sure that operation mode as compulsory.

5. Click on Remote client list edit and click rows as 1, type client node name as WHSB_Atlanta_US.

6. Click Ok.

7. Click on the row 2 tunnel source name edit type as Tokyo_Router and then click on tunnel destination name edit type as HQ_Router.

8. Make sure that operation mode as compulsory.

9. Click on Remote client list edit and click rows as 2, type client node name as WHSB_Tokyo_Japan.

10. Click Ok three times.

11. Click on go to parent subnet from toolbar.

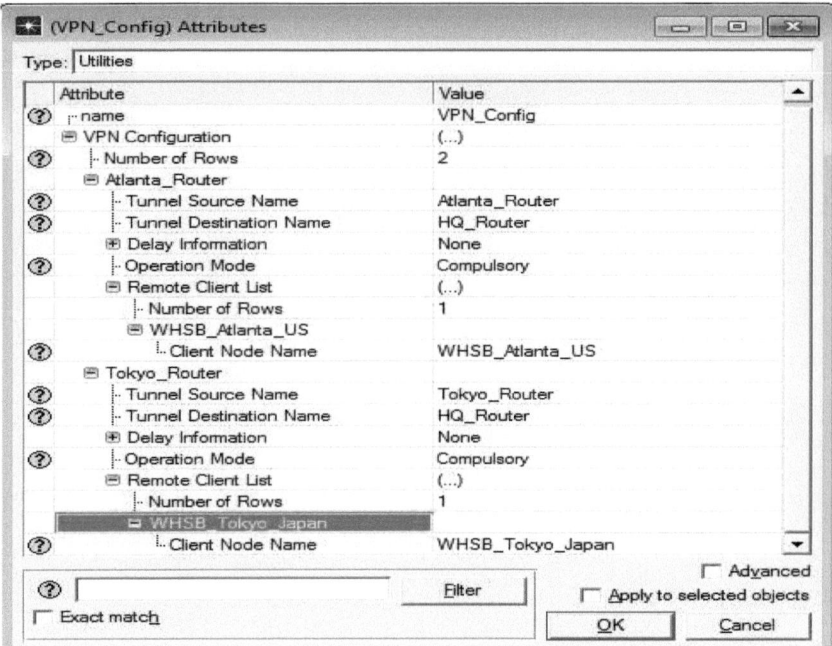

Dileep Keshava Narayana   dileep007k@gmail.com

3.1.6 WHSB_Atlanta_US

1. Double-click on the WHSB_Atlanta_US subnet, Select View > Background > Set properties and Set units to Meters. Uncheck checkbox for Satellite orbits.

2. Drag and Place one AS_GRF1600_16S_A4_AE24_F12_SLI6 router, one ethernet_slip8_gtwy_adv, one ip32_cloud, one Ethernet_printer_adv, and one Ethernet_server_adv from object palette.

3. Rename AS_GRF1600_16S_AE24_F12_SLI6 router, ethernet_slip8_gtwy_adv, ip32_cloud, Ethernet_printer_adv and ethernet_server_adv as Atlanta_Router, Atlanta_Firewall, Atlanta_Internet, Atlanta_Printer and Atlanta_Workgroup_Server respectively.

4. Now go to topology menu > Rapid configuration > star configuration and click Next.

5. Select center node model as ethernet64_switch_adv, periphery node model as ethernet_wkstn_adv, and link model as 100baseT_adv.

6. Type number as 30 as we need 30 users.

7. Click ok.

8. This create 30 users connected to switch with 100 base T link, as it is connected with 100 base T link to switch, switch will become 100 base T switch.

9. Right click on each node and rename as User 1 to User 30 for 30 nodes respectively.

10. Right click on the ethernet64_switch_adv and set name as Atlanta_switch.

11. Connect Atlanta_Printer, Atlanta_Workgroup_Server, Atlanta_Router to Atlanta_Switch and to with 100baseT_adv link from object palette.

12. Connect Atlanta_Router to Atlanta_Firewall with T1 link from object palette.

13. Connect Atlanta_Firewall to Atlanta_Internet with T1 link from object palette.

14. Click on go to parent subnet from toolbar.

6

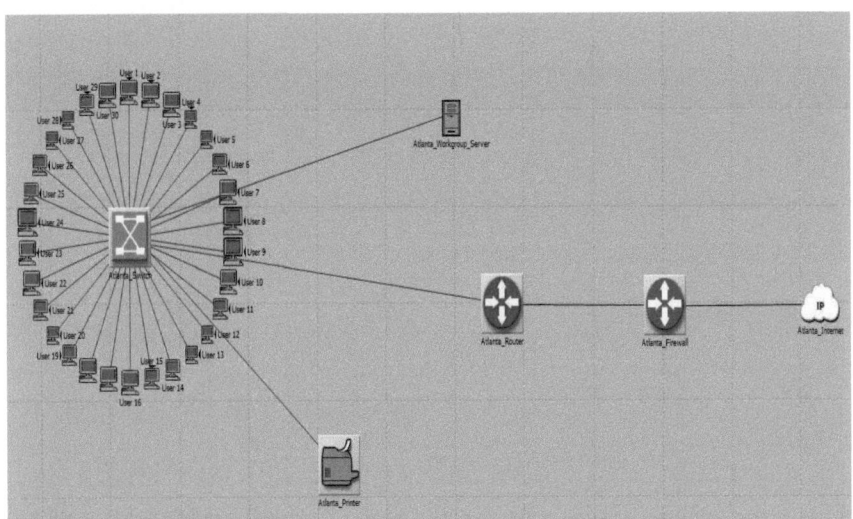

3.1.7 WHSB_Tokyo_Japan Subnet

1. Double-click on the WHSB_Tokyo_Japan subnet, Select View > Background > Set properties and Set units to Meters. Uncheck checkbox for Satellite orbits.

2. Drag and Place one AS_GRF1600_16S_A4_AE24_F12_SLI6 router, one ethernet_slip8_gtwy_adv, one ip32_cloud, one Ethernet_printer_adv, and one Ethernet_server_adv from object palette.

3. Rename AS_GRF1600_16S_AE24_F12_SLI6 router, ethernet_slip8_gtwy_adv, ip32_cloud, Ethernet_printer_adv and ethernet_server_adv as Tokyo_Router, Tokyo_Firewall, Tokyo_Internet, Tokyo_Printer and Tokyo_Workgroup_Server respectively.

4. Now go to topology menu > Rapid configuration > star configuration and click Next.

5. Select center node model as ethernet64_switch_adv, periphery node model as ethernet_wkstn_adv, and link model as 100baseT_adv.

6. Type number as 25 as we need 25 users.

7. Click ok

8. This create 25 users connected to switch with 100 base T link, as it is connected with 100 base T link to switch, switch will become 100 base T switch.

9. Right click on each node and rename as User 1 to User 25 for 25 nodes respectively.

7

10. Right click on the ethernet64_switch_adv and set name as Tokyo_switch.

11. Connect Tokyo_Printer, Tokyo_Workgroup_Server, Tokyo_Router to Tokyo_Switch and to with 100baseT_adv link from object palette.

12. Connect Tokyo_Router to Tokyo_Firewall with T1 link from object palette.

13. Connect Tokyo_Firewall to Tokyo_Internet with T1 link from object palette.

14. Click on go to parent subnet from toolbar.

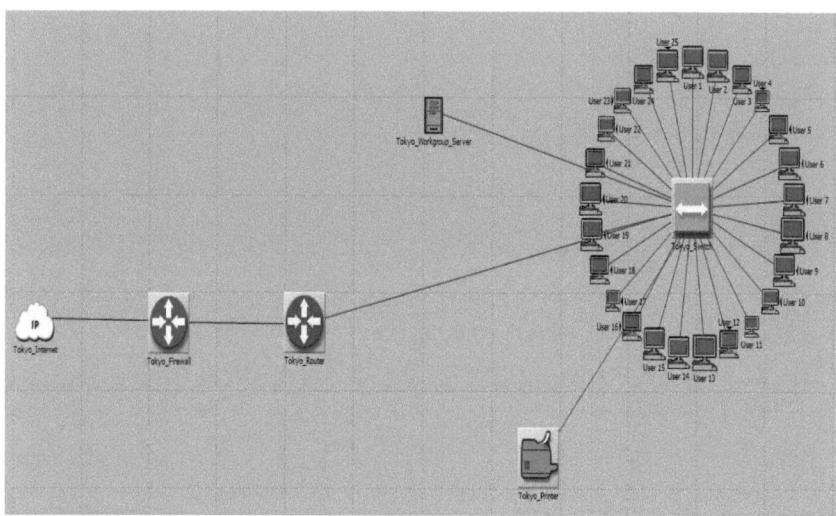

3.1.8 Connecting subnets with T1 link

1. Select T1 link from object palette. Connect WHSB_London_UK_HQ subnet to WHSB_Atlanta_US subnet. You will be asked to select nodes. Select Node a as WHSB_London_UK_HQ.HQ_Router and Node b as WHSB_Atlanta_US.Atlanta_Router

2. Connect WHSB_London_UK_HQ subnet to WHSB_Tokyo_Japan subnet. You will be asked to select nodes. Select Node a as WHSB_London_UK_HQ.HQ_Router and Node b as WHSB_Tokyo_Japan.Tokyo_Router.

Dileep Keshava Narayana   dileep007k@gmail.com

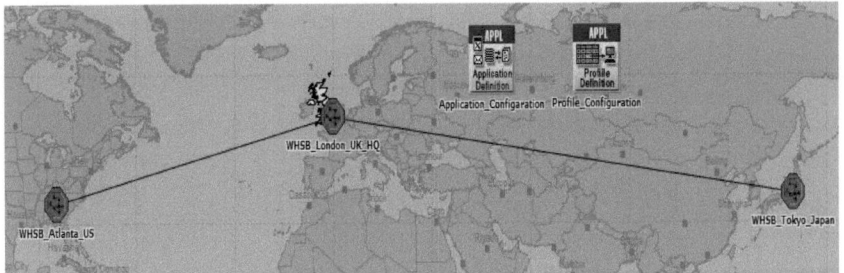

Now the subnets are connected. Subnets must be connected to router as we are making use of firewall and VPN. Once we connect to router, router knows the other subnet's router address to forward the packets to destination.

3.1.9 Application Configuration

Application can be any common application such as email, file transfer, database, telnet, video conferencing, print, voice conferencing.

As all services like (FTP, webbrowsing and the like) will be supported in the WHSB_London_UK_HQ (Headquarters office) we need one Application configuration to configure application services in general

1. Place one Application config from object palette in map.

2. Right click on Application config, select edit attributes, click on name and type as Application_Configuration.

3. Click on Application definition > edit.

4. Click on rows, select edit, and type 8 rows.

5. Click and type on first row Application Name as WebBrowsing. Click on description edit, In Http description value select Heavy Browsing. Click Ok.

6. Click and type on second row Application Name as FTP. Click on description edit, In Ftp description value select Low Load. Click Ok.

7. Click and type on third row Application Name as Email. Click on description edit, In Email description value select High Load. Click Ok.

8. Click and type on fourth row Application Name as Printer. Click on description edit, In Print description value select Text File. Click Ok.

9. Click and type on fifth row Application Name as Database (Light). Click on description edit, In Database description value select Low Load. Click Ok.

9

10. Click and type on sixth row Application Name as Database (Heavy). Click on description edit, In Database description value select High Load. Click Ok.

11. Click and type on seventh row Application Name as Video_Conferencing. Click on description edit, In Video Conferencing description value select High Resolution Video. Click Ok.

12. Click and type on first row Application Name as Voice_Conferencing. Click on description edit, In Voice description value select PCM Quality Speech. Click Ok two times.

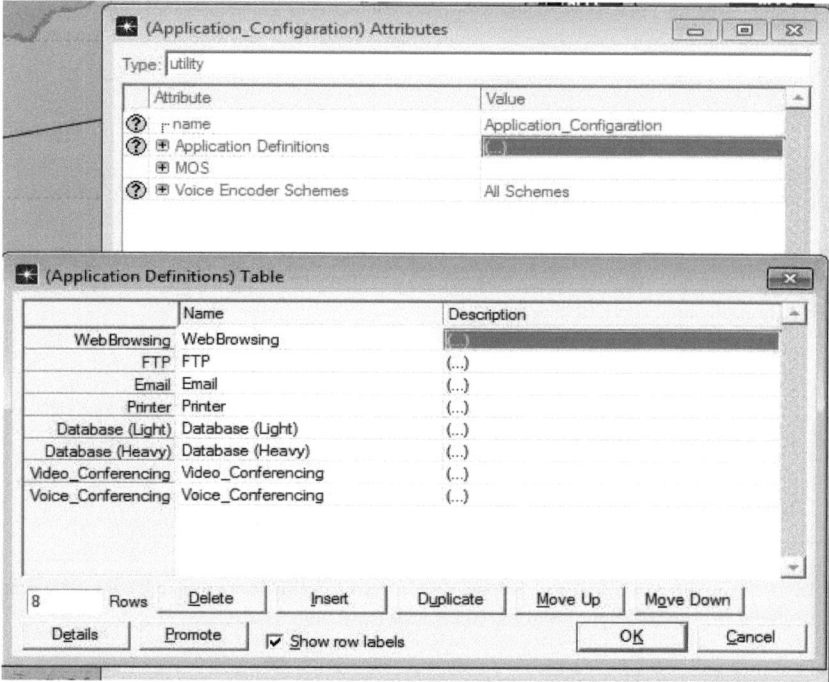

Now the applications are configured. Next step is configuring profiles.

3.1.10 Profile Configuration

Profile specifies the applications used by the particular group of users and is applicable to a workstation, server or LAN. There are can be more than one profiles depending upon the description value of use. Profile configuration is used to generate traffic.

1. Place one Profile config from object palette in map.

2. Right click on Profile config, select edit attributes, click on name and type as Profile_Configuration.

3. Click on Profile Configuration > edit.

4. Click on rows, select edit, and type 7 rows.

5. Click and type on first row Profile Name as Web_browsing. Click on Applications edit, select 1 row, Select Application name as WebBrowsing, In start time offset select distribution name as constant and mean outcome as 100. Click Ok 2 times.

6. Click and type on second row Profile Name as FTP. Click on Applications edit, select 1 row, Select Application name as FTP. In start time offset select distribution name as constant and mean outcome as 100. Click Ok 2 times.

7. Click and type on third row Profile Name as Database. Click on Applications edit, select 2 rows, Select Application names as Database (Light) and Database (Heavy) in first and second row respectively. In start time offset select distribution name as constant and mean outcome as 100. Click Ok 2 times.

8. Click and type on fourth row Profile Name as Video_Conferencing. Click on Applications edit, select 1 row, Select Application name as Video_Conferencing, In start time offset select distribution name as constant and mean outcome as 100. Click Ok 2 times.

9. Click and type on fifth row Profile Name as Voice_Conferencing. Click on Applications edit, select 1 row, Select Application name as Voice_Conferencing, In start time offset select distribution name as constant and mean outcome as 100. Click Ok 2 times.

10. Click and type on sixth row Profile Name as Printer. Click on Applications edit, select 1 row, Select Application name as Printer, In start time offset select distribution name as constant and mean outcome as 100. Click Ok 2 times.

11. Click and type on seventh row Profile Name as Email. Click on Applications edit, select 1 row, Select Application name as Email, In start time offset select distribution name as constant and mean outcome as 100. Click Ok 3 times.

Now the profiles are configured. Next step is assigning profiles.

Dileep Keshava Narayana   dileep007k@gmail.com

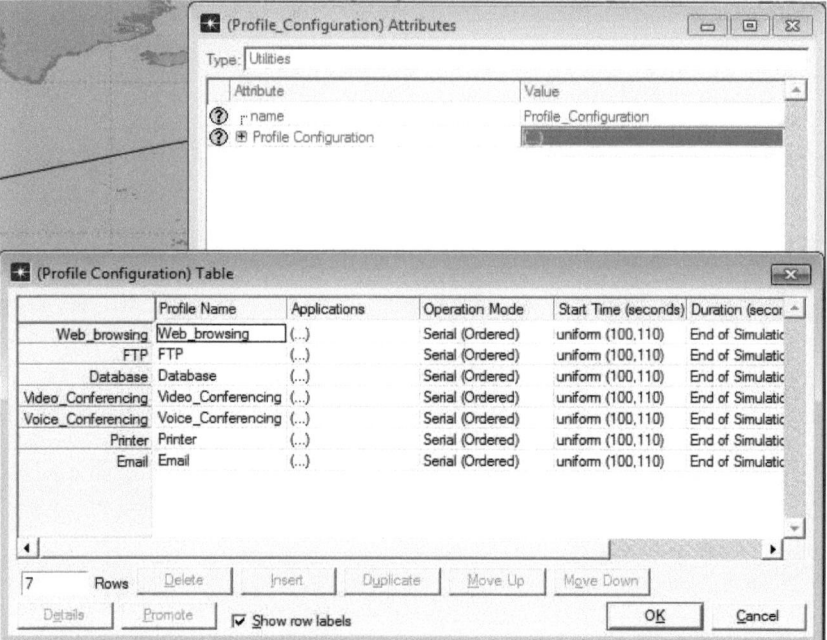

3.1.11 Assigning Profiles: Assigning Services to WHSB_London_UK_HQ Servers.

First lets assign the supported services to the servers in the WHSB_London_UK_HQ.

1. Now double click on WHSB_London_UK_HQ subnet.

2. Right click on Web_Server_HQ. Select edit attributes, go to applications > Application supported services, click edit, Select 1 rows, Select the name in application supported services table as WebBrowsing. Click Ok 2 times.

3. Right click on Database_Server_HQ. Select edit attributes, go to applications > Application supported services, click edit, Select 1 rows, Select the name in application supported services table as Database (Heavy) ..Click Ok 2 times.

4. Right click on FTP_Server_HQ. Select edit attributes, go to applications > Application supported services, click edit, Select 1 rows, Select the name in application supported services table as FTP. Click Ok 2 times.

5. Right click on Email_Server_HQ. Select edit attributes, go to applications > Application supported services, click edit, Select 1 rows, Select the name in application supported services table as Email. Click Ok 2 times.

12

6. Right click on Conference_Server_HQ. Select edit attributes, go to applications > Application supported services, click edit, Select 2 rows, Select names in application supported services table as Video_Conferencing and Voice_Conferencing in first and second row respectively.. Click Ok 2 times.

7. Click on go to parent subnet from toolbar.

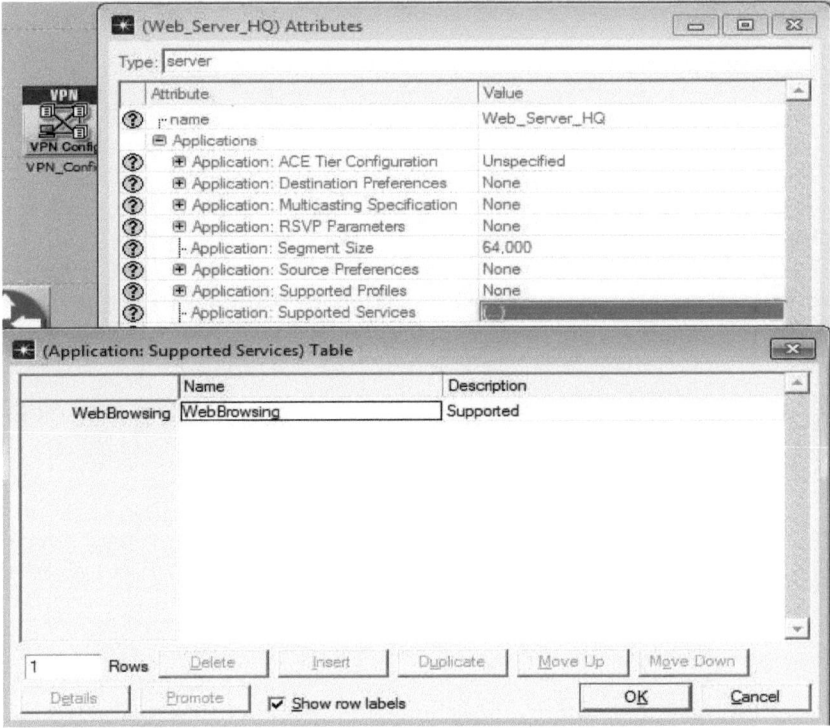

The motive of creating separate servers for the services such as Webbrowsing, FTP, Email, Database, and Conference in the Headquarters London UK is to provide additional security to the organization network. It also increases network performance and makes it easy to access the services such as FTP, Web browsing, Emails, voice and video conferencing services if employee of Headquarters visits the other branches of organization in Atlanta or Tokyo.

Now the servers in Headquarters are assigned to provide the services to other branches. Next step is to configure the workgroup server in Atlanta and Tokyo to provide the services locally with in the branch and to synchronize the information from the Headquarters servers.

As the Services such as Database (Light), Email, and Printing are provided locally within the branch of Atlanta. We need to assign the services for the workgroup servers to provide

13

services such as Database (Light) and Email locally. We will also assign the profile for the printing, Email and Database (Heavy) to the workgroup server in Atlanta. As we need to store the printing information locally in the server. We will synchronize the Emails to the Headquarters server so that it can be easily accessed from any branch for the employees. We will assign Database (Heavy) Profile to the workgroup server in Atlanta, So that the workgroup servers in Atlanta could obtain and store the information from the Database (Heavy) located in Headquarters in London. This helps to gather, store and distribute sales reports among all branches.

As the Services such as Database (Heavy), Email, and Printing are provided locally within the branch of Tokyo. We need to assign the services for the workgroup servers to provide services such as Database (Heavy) and Email locally. We will also assign the profile for the printing, Email and Database (Light) to the workgroup server in Tokyo. As we need to store the printing information locally in the server. We will synchronize the Emails to the Headquarters server so that it can be easily accessed from any branch for the employees. We will assign Database (Light) and Database (Heavy) Profiles to the workgroup server in Tokyo, So that the workgroup servers in Tokyo could also obtain and store the information from the Database (Heavy) and Database (Light) located in Headquarters in London and Atlanta. This helps to gather, store and distribute sales reports among all branches.

3.1.12 Assigning Services and Profiles to WHSB_Atlanta_US and WHSB_Tokyo_Japan Workgroup servers.

1. Now double click on WHSB_Atlanta_US subnet.

2. Right click on Atlanta_Workgroup_Server. Select edit attributes, go to applications > Application supported services, click edit, Select 2 rows, Select names in application supported services table as Database (Light) and Email in first and second row respectively. Click Ok.

3. Now click on edit in Application Supported Profiles, Select 3 rows, Select Profile names as Database, Printer, and Email in first, second and third row respectively. Click Ok 2 times.

4. Click on go to parent subnet from toolbar.

5. Now double click on WHSB_Tokyo_Japan subnet.

6. Right click on Tokyo_Workgroup_Server. Select edit attributes, go to applications > Application supported services, click edit, Select 2 rows, Select names in application supported services table as Database (Heavy) and Email in first and second row respectively. Click Ok.

7. Now click on edit in Application Supported Profiles, Select 3 rows, Select Profile names as Database, Printer, and Email in first, second and third row respectively. Click Ok 2 times.

14

8. Click on go to parent subnet from toolbar.

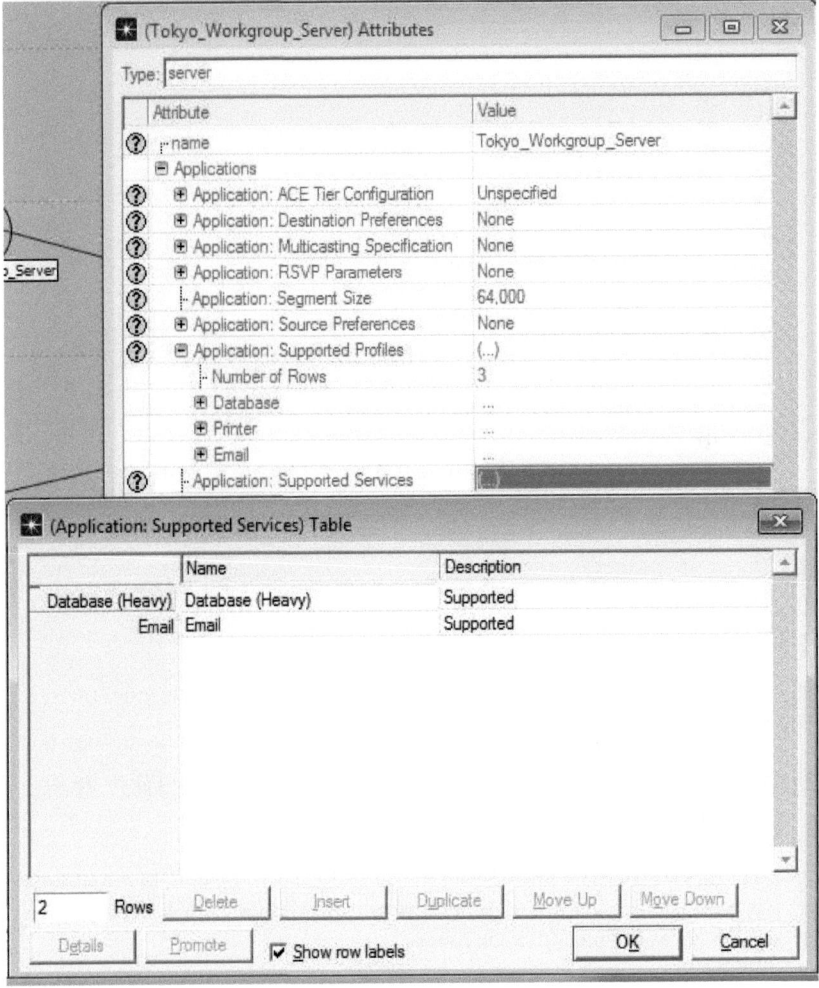

Dileep Keshava Narayana   dileep007k@gmail.com

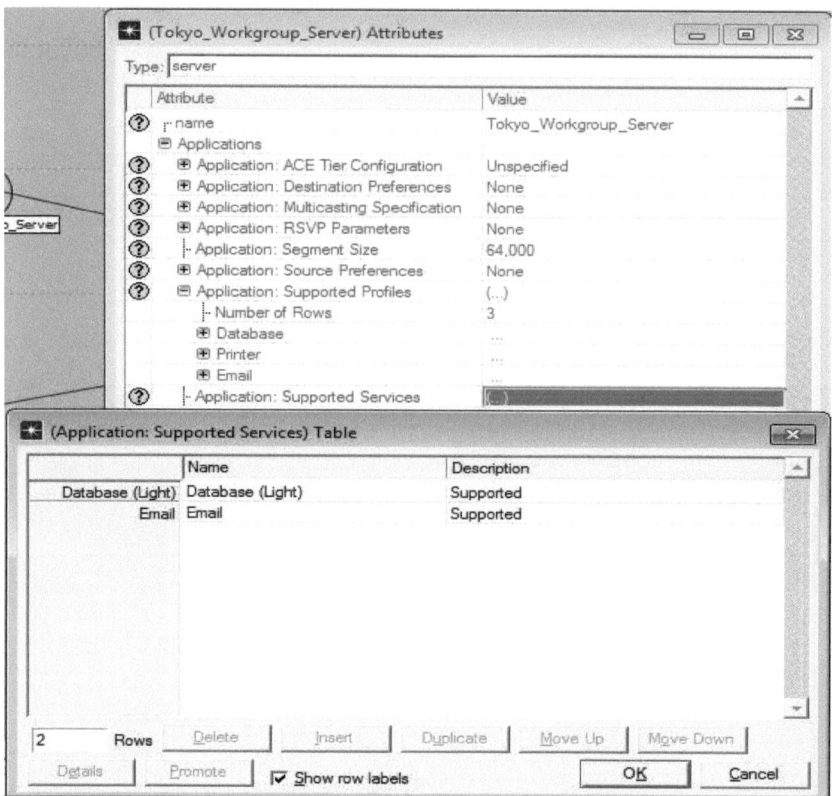

3.1.13 Assigning Services to printer in WHSB_Atlanta_US and WHSB_Tokyo_Japan

1. Now double click on WHSB_Atlanta_US subnet.

2. Right click on Atlanta_Printer. Select edit attributes, go to applications > Application supported services, click edit, Select 1 rows, Select name in application supported services table as Printer. Click Ok 2 times.

3. Click on go to parent subnet from toolbar.

4. Now double click on WHSB_Tokyo_Japan subnet.

5. Right click on Tokyo_Printer. Select edit attributes, go to applications > Application supported services, click edit, Select 1 rows, Select name in application supported services table as Printer. Click Ok 2 times.

6. Click on go to parent subnet from toolbar.

Dileep Keshava Narayana   dileep007k@gmail.com

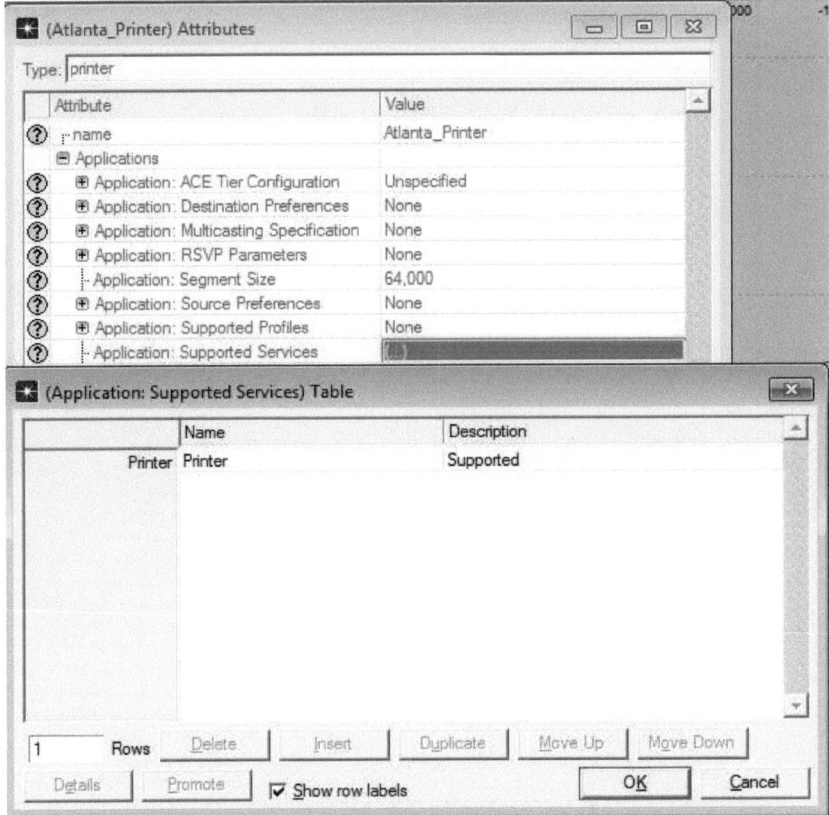

3.1.14 Assigning Profiles to users in WHSB_Atlanta_US and WHSB_Tokyo_Japan

1. Now double click on WHSB_Atlanta_US subnet.

2. Select User 1 to User 10, Right click on any User, Select edit attributes, go to applications > Application supported profiles, click edit, Select 6 rows, Select Profile names Web_browsing, FTP, Database, Printer, Email, Video_Conferencing in first, second, third, fourth, fifth and sixth rows respectively. Click Ok. Check mark Apply to selected objects, Click Ok again.

3. Select User 11 to User 30, Right click on any User, Select edit attributes, go to applications > Application supported profiles, click edit, Select 5 rows, Select Profile names Web_browsing, FTP, Database, Printer, Email in first, second, third, fourth, and fifth rows respectively. Click Ok. Check mark Apply to selected objects, Click Ok again.

17

4. Click on go to parent subnet from toolbar.

5. Now double click on WHSB_Tokyo_Japan subnet.

6. Select User 1 to User 10, Right click on any User, Select edit attributes, go to applications > Application supported profiles, click edit, Select 7 rows, Select Profile names Web_browsing, FTP, Database, Printer, Email, Video_Conferencing and Voice_Conferencing in first, second, third, fourth, fifth, sixth, seventh rows respectively. Click Ok. Check mark Apply to selected objects, Click Ok again.

7. Select User 11 to User 25, Right click on any User, Select edit attributes, go to applications > Application supported profiles, click edit, Select 5 rows, Select Profile names Web_browsing, FTP, Database, Printer, Email in first, second, third, fourth, and fifth rows respectively. Click Ok. Check mark Apply to selected objects, Click Ok again.

8. Click on go to parent subnet from toolbar.

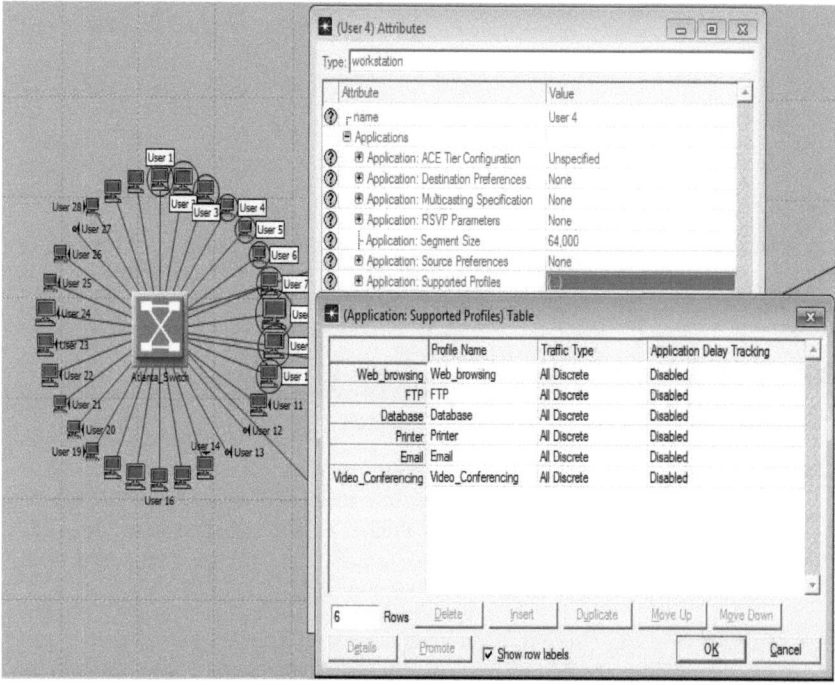

Now User 1 to User 10 in Atlanta can run Online Video conferencing application. In Tokyo User 1 to User 10 can run Voice and video conferencing applications.

This completes the scenario 1 model.

18

3.2 Scenario 2

3.2.1 Duplicate Scenario

To duplicate scenario go to scenario menu, click duplicate scenario, Enter the name as cs2.

3.2.2 WHSB_Atlanta_US Subnet

1. Double click on WHSB_Atlanta_US subnet.

2. Select User 1 to User 30, and all 100 base T_adv links connected to Atlanta_Switch of User 1 to User 30.

3. This retains Atlanta_printer connected with 100 base T_adv link to Atlanta_Switch and Atlanta_Switch.

4. Go to Topology menu > Rapid configuration. Select Rapid Configuration as star topology, click Next.

5. Select center node model as ethernet32_hub_adv, periphery node model as ethernet_wkstn_adv, and link model as 100baseT_adv.

6. Type number as 20 as we need 20 users connected to one hub.

7. Click ok.

8. This creates 20 users connected to hub with 100 base T link.

9. Right click on each node and rename as User 1 to User 20 for 20 nodes respectively.

10. Go to Topology menu > Rapid configuration. Select Rapid Configuration as star topology, click Next.

11. Select center node model as ethernet16_hub_adv, periphery node model as ethernet_wkstn_adv, and link model as 100baseT_adv.

12. Type number as 10 as we need 10 users connected to one hub.

13. Click ok.

14. This creates 10 users connected to hub with 100 base T link.

15. Right click on each node and rename as User 21 to User 30 for 10 nodes respectively.

16. Right click on ethernet32_hub_adv, set name as Atlanta_Hub1.

17. Right click on ethernet16_hub_adv, set name as Atlanta_Hub2.

18. Connect Atlanta_Hub1 and Atlanta_Hub2 with 100 base T_adv link to Atlanta_Switch.

19

19. Select User 21 to User 30, Right click > Select edit attributes > Applications > Click on Application supported profiles.

20. Select edit, Click on rows, select edit and type as 6 rows.

21. Type name in first, second, third, fourth, fifth and sixth rows profile name as Web_browsing, FTP, Database, Printer, Email, and Video_Conferencing. Click ok. Check mark Apply to selected objects then click Ok.

22. Now select User 1 to User 20, Right click > Select edit attributes > Applications > Click on Application supported profiles.

23. Select edit, Click on rows, select edit and type as 6 rows.

24. Type name in first, second, third, fourth, fifth and sixth rows profile name as Web_browsing, FTP, Database, Printer, and Email. Click ok. Check mark Apply to selected objects then click Ok.

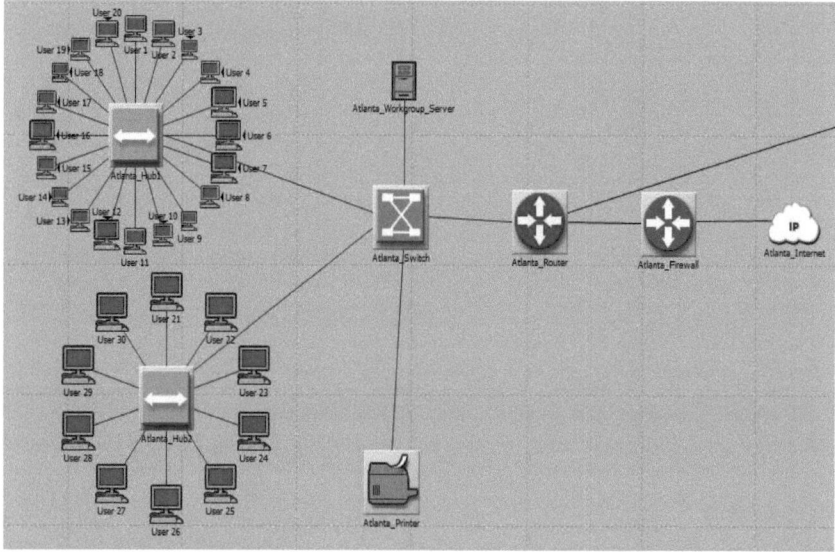

The motive of separating 10 users, 20 users with hub and then connecting it to switch is to provide differentiated the services. As 10 users are using video conferencing applications grouping them together, it makes the tasks easy for administrator to maintain the systems in the network for the administration and to maintain the logs.

3.2.3 WHSB_Tokyo_Japan Subnet

1. Double click on WHSB_Tokyo_Japan subnet.

2. Select User 1 to User 25, and all 10 base T_adv links connected to Tokyo_Switch of User 1 to User 25.

3. This retains Tokyo_printer connected with 10 base T_adv link to Tokyo_Switch and Tokyo_Switch.

4. Go to Topology menu > Rapid configuration. Select Rapid Configuration as star topology, click Next.

5. Select center node model as ethernet16_hub_adv, periphery node model as ethernet_wkstn_adv, and link model as 10 baseT_adv.

6. Type number as 15 as we need 15 users connected to one hub.

7. Click ok.

8. This creates 15 users connected to hub with 10 base T link.

9. Right click on each node and rename as User 1 to User 15 for 15 nodes respectively.

10. Go to Topology menu > Rapid configuration. Select Rapid Configuration as star topology, click Next.

11. Select center node model as ethernet16_hub_adv, periphery node model as ethernet_wkstn_adv, and link model as 10 baseT_adv.

12. Type number as 10 as we need 10 users connected to one hub.

13. Click ok.

14. This creates 10 users connected to hub with 100 base T link.

15. Right click on each node and rename as User 16 to User 25 for 10 nodes respectively.

16. Right click on ethernet16_hub_adv, set name as Tokyo_Hub1.

17. Right click on ethernet16_hub_adv, set name as Tokyo_Hub2.

18. Connect Tokyo_Hub1 and Tokyo_Hub2 with 10 base T_adv link to Tokyo_Switch.

19. Select User 16 to User 25, Right click > Select edit attributes > Applications > Click on Application supported profiles.

20. Select edit, Click on rows, select edit and type as 7 rows.

21. Type name in first, second, third, fourth, fifth sixth, and seventh rows profile name as Web_browsing, FTP, Database, Printer, Email, Voice_Conferencing and Video_Conferencing. Click ok. Check mark Apply to selected objects then click Ok.

21

22. Now select User 1 to User 15, Right click > Select edit attributes > Applications > Click on Application supported profiles.

23. Select edit, Click on rows, select edit and type as 6 rows.

24. Type name in first, second, third, fourth, fifth and sixth rows profile name as Web_browsing, FTP, Database, Printer, and Email. Click ok. Check mark Apply to selected objects then click Ok.

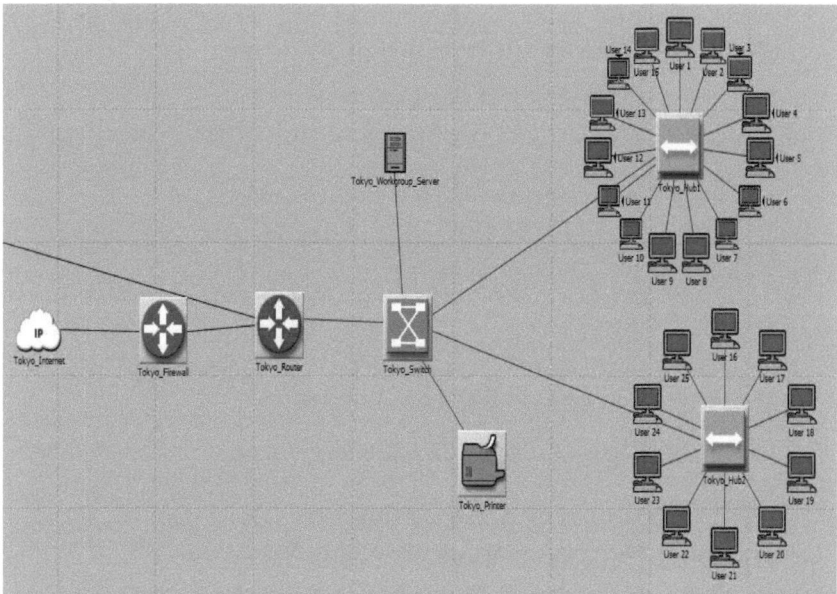

The motive of separating 10 users, 20 users with hub and then connecting it to switch is to provide differentiated the services. As 10 users are using video conferencing and voice conferencing applications grouping them together, it makes the tasks easy for administrator to maintain the systems in the network for the administration and to maintain the logs.

4. Simulating the scenarios

4.1 Collecting Statistics

1. The configuration of both scenarios is complete. To run the simulation we need to choose the statistics to be collected. Steps below explain configuring the statistics to be collected.

2. Right click in the workspace. Select Choose Individual DES statistics.

22

3. In Global statistics > Ethernet: check mark Delay (Sec), in Ftp: Check mark Download Response Time (Sec), in Http: Object Response Time (Seconds), in Voice & Video Conferencing: Check mark Packet Delay Variation, Packet End to end Delay (Sec), Traffic Received (Packets/Sec), and Traffic sent (Packets/sec).

4. In Link Statistics > point-to-point, check mark utilization -> and utilization <-.

5. Click Ok.

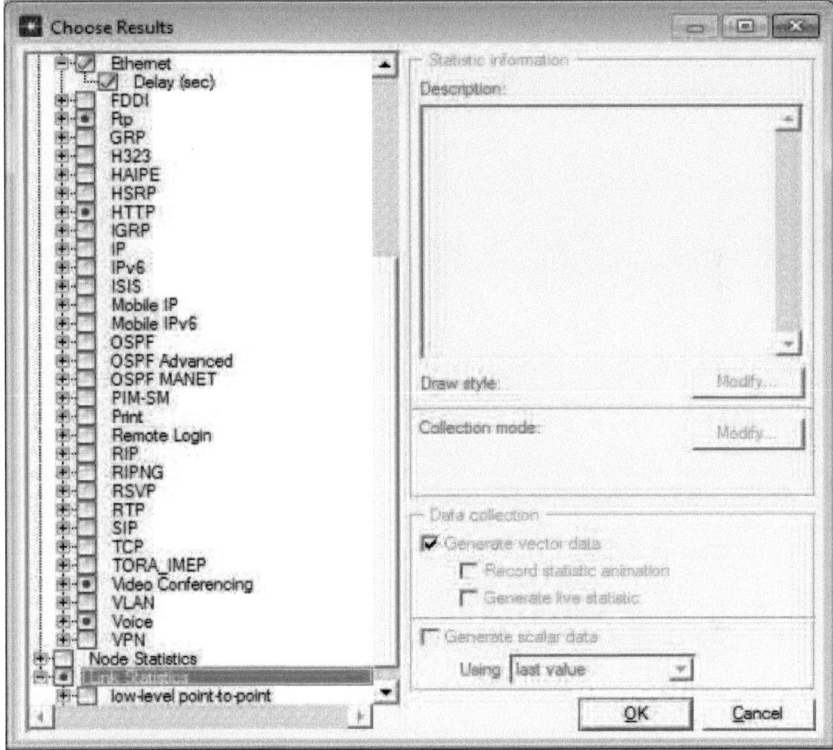

4.2 Running Simulation

1. Go to Edit menu > Preferences.

2. Search as network sim. Click on Network simulation Repositories value. Click on <empty> and then on insert. Type as stdmod. Click ok 2 times.

3. Go to DES menu > Select Configure/ Run Discrete Event Simulation.

4. Make Duration as 1 Hour. Update interval 10000 events, and select Simulation kernel as optimized. Click on apply and then click on cancel.

23

5. Save the project.

6. Go to Scenarios > Manage Scenarios. Select Results for cs1 and cs2 scenario names as collect.

7. Click Ok.

Simulation will be launched. Wait until the simulation is completed.

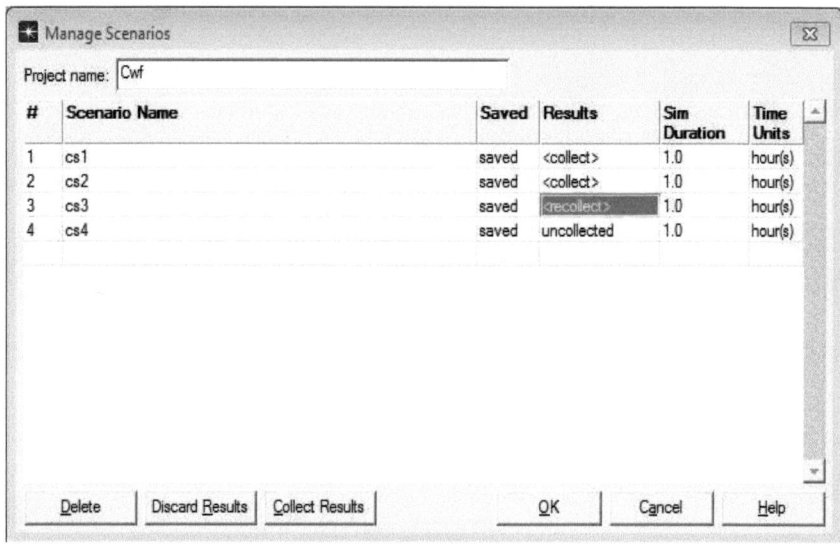

Dileep Keshava Narayana   dileep007k@gmail.com

4.3 Results

1. Once the simulation is completed, Right click in workspace, Click on view results.

2. In Results browser for select Current project, select cs1 and cs2 scenarios.

3. To compare results from two scenarios, Select Overlaid Statistics and average.

4. Select the components which need to be investigated from global and object statistics.

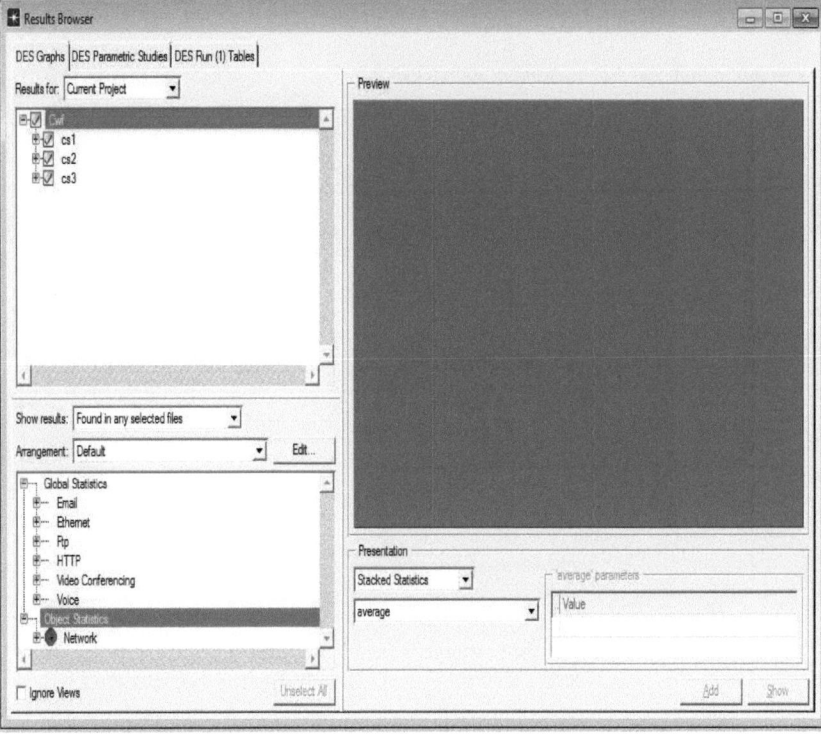

5. Investigation

From results obtained we can investigate the following:

5.1 Utilization of T1 link

To investigate T1 link, go to Results browser > Object statistics > WHSB_London_UK_HQ > HQ_Firewall <-> HQ_Internet [0] > point-to-point > Select utilization <-, WHSB_Atlanta_US > Atlanta_Firewall <-> Atlanta_Internet [0] > point-to-point > Select utilization <-, and WHSB_Tokyo_Japan > Tokyo_Firewall <-> Tokyo_Internet [0] > point-to-point > Select utilization <-.

The resulting graph should resemble as shown below:

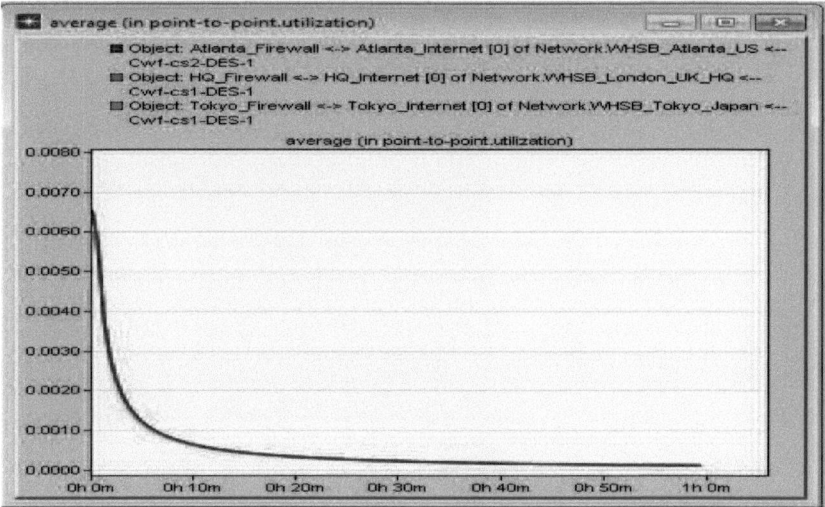

By the graph we can analyse that average utilization of the T1 link is exponentially decreasing with time from 0.0065 for all subnets and for both scenario 1 & scenario 2..

Finally, utilization of the T1 link is low. We can still accommodate some more users and services.

I did not expect the utilization of the T1 link to be low, however by accommodating some more users, services and connecting with 1000 base T links or higher to users and switch can increase the T1 link utilization.

26

5.2 Average FTP download response time

To investigate average FTP download response time, go to Results browser > Global statistics > Ftp > Select download response time (sec).

The resulting graph should resemble as shown below:

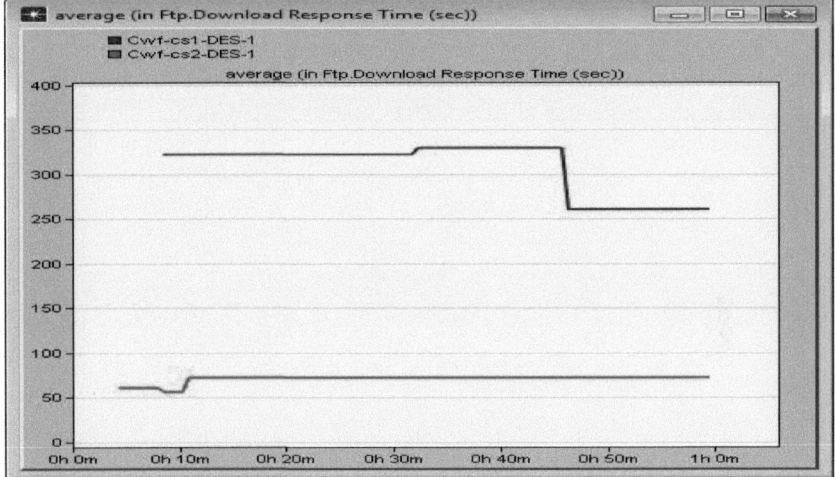

By the above graph we can analyse that in scenario 1 the average FTP download response time is high starting from 350 seconds of the connection and by the end of connection it is reduced to 260 seconds.

In scenario 2, the average FTP download response time is low starting from 52 seconds and increases slight, remains constant till the end of the connection.

Finally, scenario 2 average FTP download response time is low than the scenario 1.

As FTP uses UDP to transfer packets, it does not provide guaranteed packet delivery service. So the packets might get disposed or lost in the network. Because of this reason FTP download response time is high.

FTP download response time can be improved by making use of cloud storage services in which the data can be accessed location independently. However WHSB organization uses low load of FTP, so it is not a wise decision to incur huge investments on it until there is high load.

27

5.3 HTTP page response time (seconds)

To investigate average HTTP page response time, go to Results browser > Global statistics > HTTP > Select page response time (seconds).

Resulting graph should resemble the following:

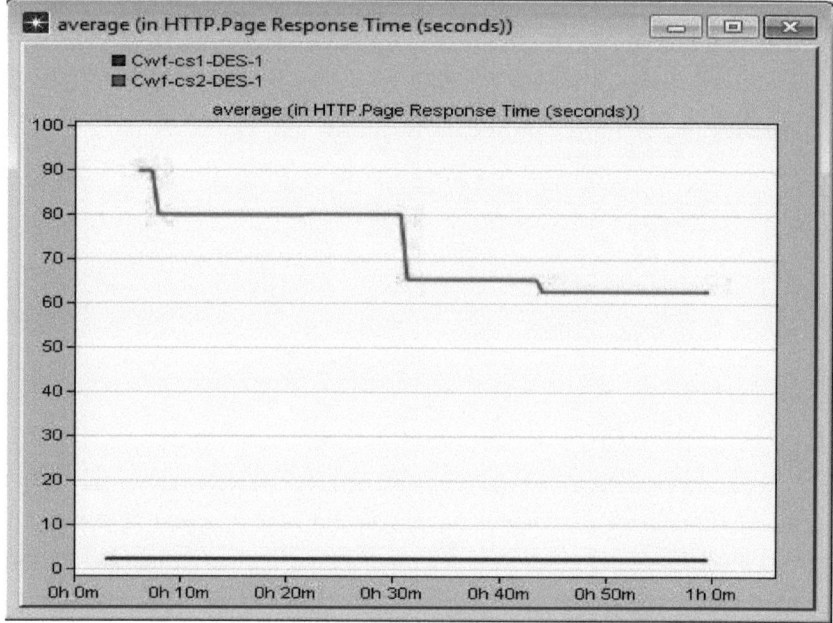

By the above we can analyse that the HTTP page response time in scenario is constantly low and in scenario 2 it is reducing lately from high value.

As HTTP is of high load, the page response time can differ greatly. The models work as expected.

HTTP page response time can be improved by increasing the utilization of T1 link. To increase the utilization of the T1 link, we need to connect the users with 1000 base T links or higher. HTTP page response time can further be improved by using ATM servers.

Dileep Keshava Narayana   dileep007k@gmail.com

5.4 Behaviour of voice and video application

Video Conferencing

Packet Delay variation

Packet delay variation is sometimes called as jitter. It is the variation of the speed with respect to some interval of time.

To investigate average Packet delay variation in video conferencing, go to Results browser > Global statistics > Video Conferencing > Select Packet delay variation.

Resulting graph should resemble the following:

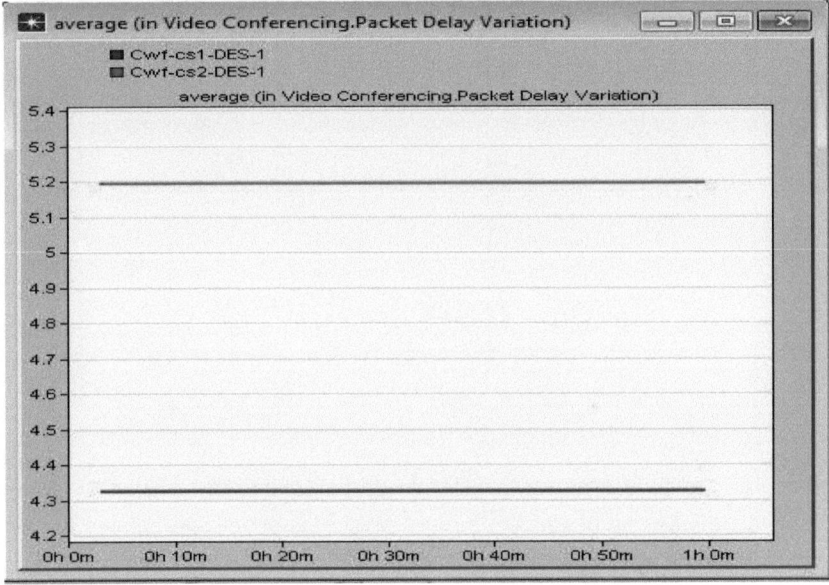

By the graph above we can analyse that, in both scenario 1 and scenario 2 packet delay variation is constant.

In scenario 1, Packet delay variation is low than in scenario 2.

As we have used firewall, firewall terminates ip stream in one side side of it and recreates it on other side. Even though this provides additional security in the network it might introduce some packet delay.

Both scenario 1 and scenario 2 works as expected.

29

Packet End-to-End Delay

Packet end to end delay is the time taken to transmit the packet from source to destination.

To investigate average Packet end to end delay in video conferencing, go to Results browser > Global statistics > Video Conferencing > Select Packet end to end delay.

Resulting graph should resemble the following:

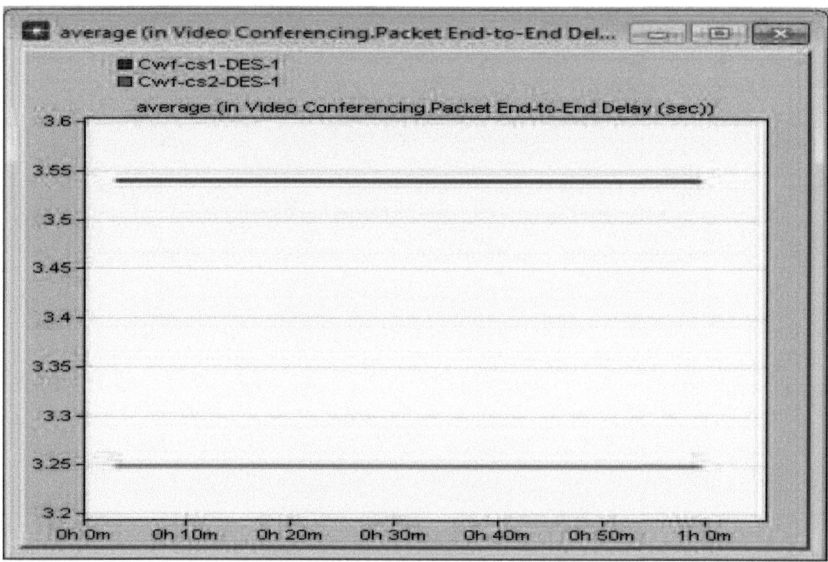

By the above graph we can analyse that the packets end to end delay in scenario 1 is more than the end to end delay in scenario 2. However, packet end to end delay in both scenarios is constant.

The models worked as expected.

30

Traffic received (Packets/ sec)

To investigate average Traffic received in video conferencing, go to Results browser > Global statistics > Video Conferencing > Select packets received.

Resulting graph should resemble the following:

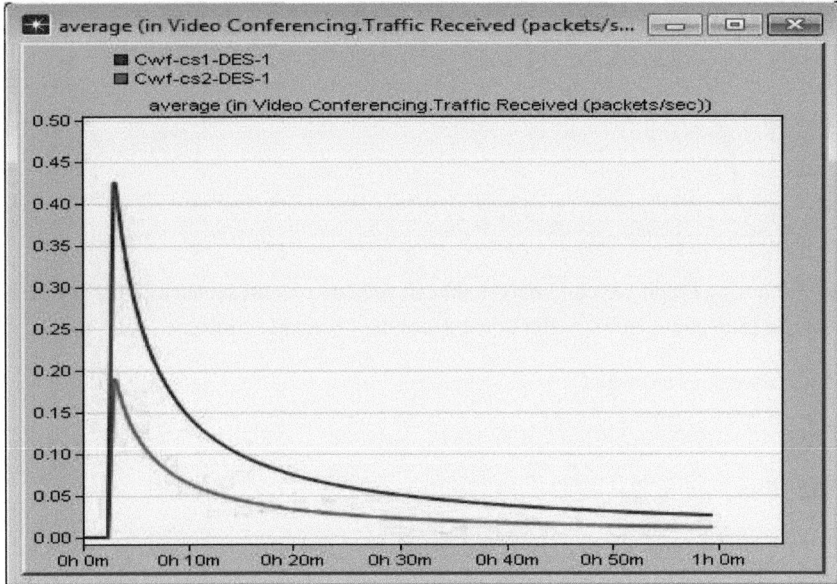

By the above graph we can analyse that the packets received in scenario 1 is more than the packets received in scenario 2.

In scenario 1, the utmost packets received are 0.42 per second.

In scenario 2, the utmost packets received are 0.18 per second.

The models work as expected.

Traffic sent (Packets/ sec)

To investigate average Traffic sent in video conferencing, go to Results browser > Global statistics > Video Conferencing > Select packets sent.

Resulting graph should resemble the following:

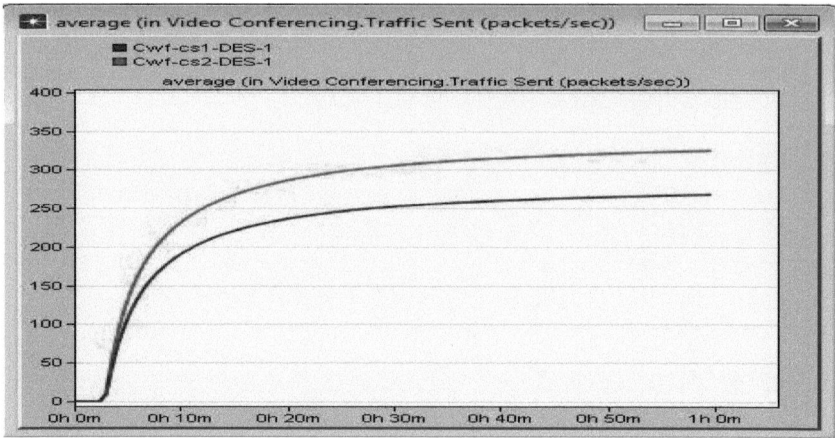

By the above graph we can analyse that in scenario 1 and scenario 2 the packets sent are increasing from 0 after some seconds it remains constant.

Models work as expected.

Voice

Jitter (Sec)

To investigate average jitter in voice conferencing, go to Results browser > Global statistics > Voice > Select Jitter (Sec).

Resulting graph should resemble the following:

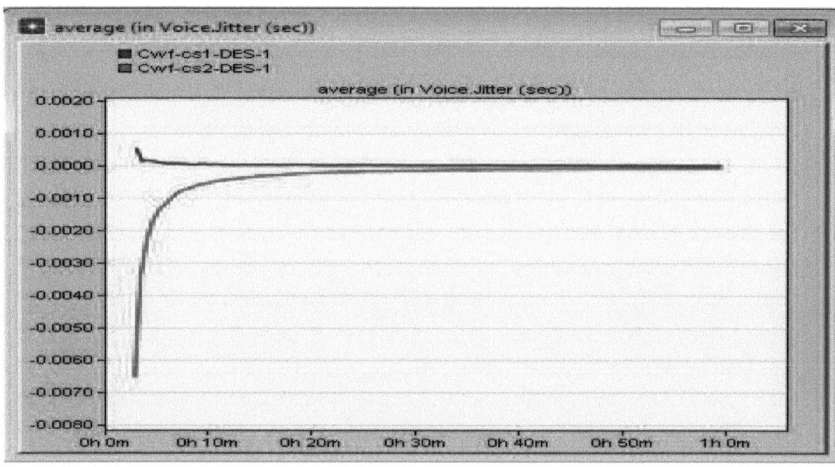

Dileep Keshava Narayana   dileep007k@gmail.com

By looking at the graph above we can analyse that the jitter is far lower for scenario 2 than scenario 1.

In scenario 1, the jitter is approximately constant starting with 0.0005.

In scenario 2, the jitter is approximately constant starting with -0.0065.

Yes model worked as expected.

MOS value

To investigate average jitter in voice conferencing, go to Results browser > Global statistics > Voice > Select MOS value.

Resulting graph should resemble the following:

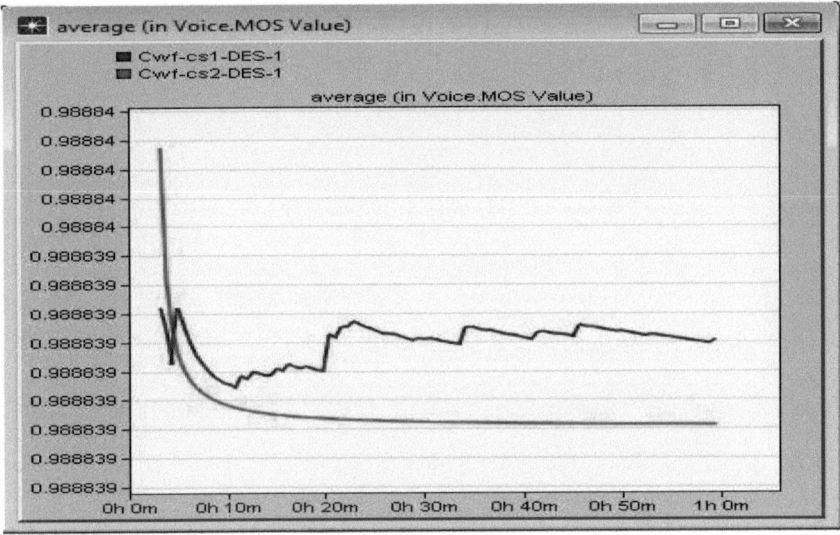

By the graph above we can analyse that in scenario 1 the MOS value is 0.988839 and in scenario 2 MOS value is 0.98884.

Dileep Keshava Narayana   dileep007k@gmail.com

Packet Delay Variation

To investigate average jitter in voice conferencing, go to Results browser > Global statistics > Voice > Select Packet delay variation (Sec).

Resulting graph should resemble the following:

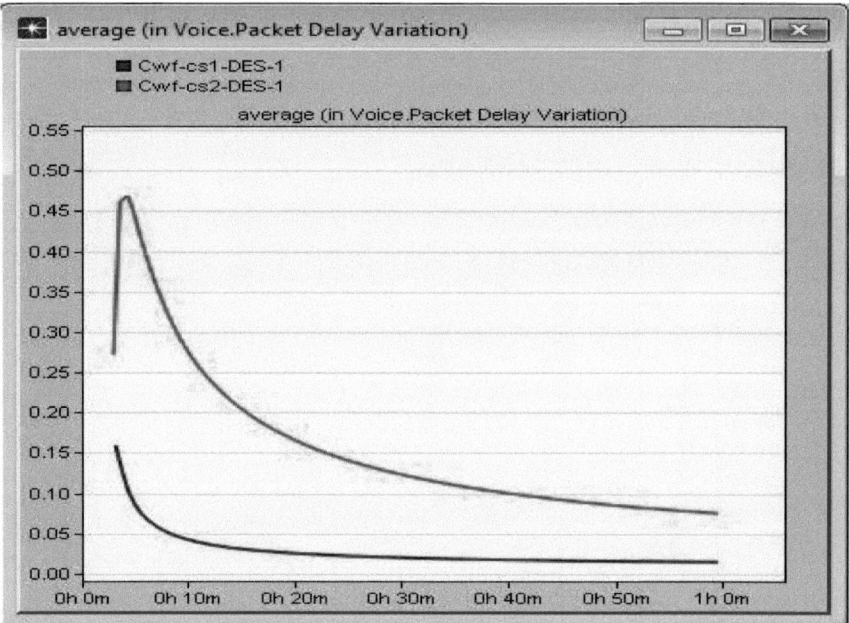

By the graph above we can analyse that in scenario 1 packet delay variation drops from 0.16 to 0 and in scenario 2 packet delay variation increases from 0.26 to 0.46 and then drops to 0.08.

So the packet delay variation is low in scenario 1 than in scenario 2.

Dileep Keshava Narayana   dileep007k@gmail.com

Packet End-to-End Delay (Sec)

To investigate average jitter in voice conferencing, go to Results browser > Global statistics > Voice > Select packet end to end delay (Sec).

Resulting graph should resemble the following:

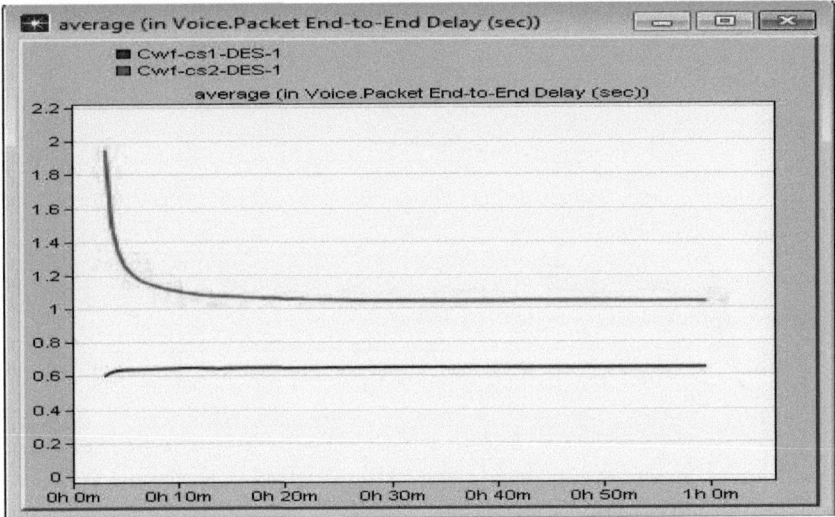

By the graph above we can analyse that packet end to end delay in scenario 1 is constant 0.6 and in scenario 2 it drops from 1.9 to 1.

Dileep Keshava Narayana   dileep007k@gmail.com

Traffic Received (Packets/ sec)

To investigate average jitter in voice conferencing, go to Results browser > Global statistics > Voice > Traffic received (Sec).

Resulting graph should resemble the following:

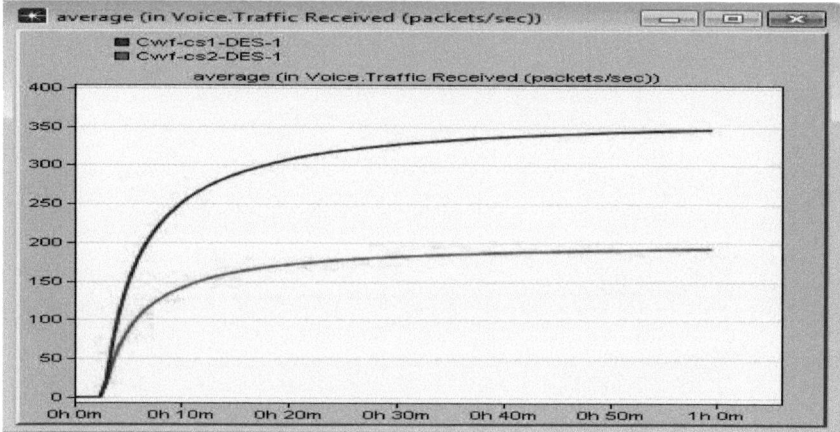

By the above graph we can analyse that traffic received in scenario 1 is higher than the traffic received in scenario 2.

Dileep Keshava Narayana   dileep007k@gmail.com

Traffic Sent (Packet/ sec)

To investigate average jitter in voice conferencing, go to Results browser > Global statistics > Voice > Select traffic sent (Sec).

Resulting graph should resemble the following:

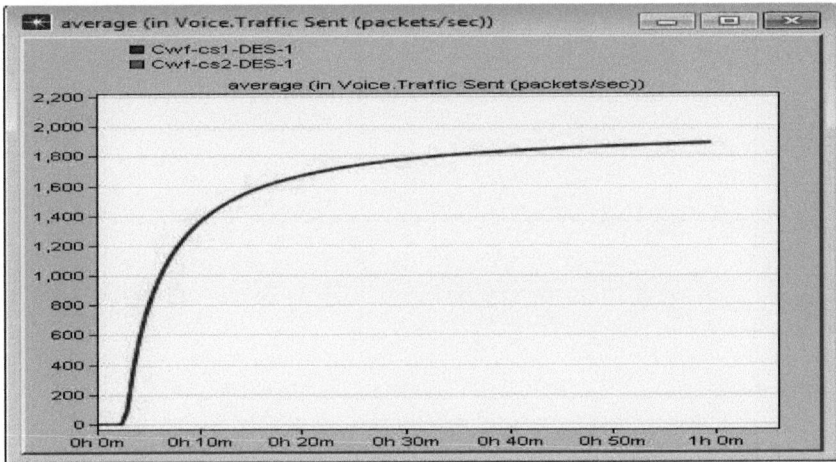

By the graph above we can analyse that the traffic sent in both scenario 1 and scenario 2 are same. It is increasing gradually.

5.5 Ethernet delay

To investigate average jitter in voice conferencing, go to Results browser > Global statistics > Ethernet > Delay (Sec).

Resulting graph should resemble the following:

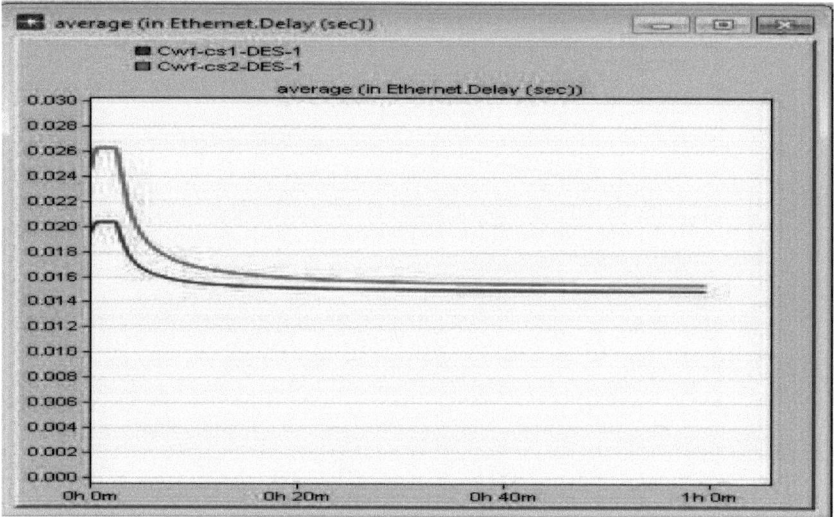

By the graph above we can analyse that the Ethernet delay in scenario 1 is lower than the Ethernet delay in scenario 2.

In scenario 1, Ethernet delay varies from 0.020 and further reduces to 0.015.

In scenario 2, Ethernet delay varies from 0.026 and further reduces to 0.0151.

So model worked as expected and Ethernet delay is low.

Dileep Keshava Narayana   dileep007k@gmail.com

5.6 New local office in Osaka, Japan & Investigation of behaviour of video conferencing application.

1. Go to scenarios menu > click on switch scenario > cs1.

2. Select Duplicate scenario from scenario menu.

3. Name scenario as cs3.

4. Open object palette, drag a subnet in Osaka.

5. Right click on Subnet, set name as WHSB_Osaka_Japan.

6. Double click on WHSB_Osaka_Japan, Select View > Background > Set properties and Set units to Meters. Uncheck checkbox for Satellite orbits.

7. Drag and Place one AS_GRF1600_16S_A4_AE24_F12_SLI6 router, one ethernet_slip8_gtwy_adv, one ip32_cloud, and one Ethernet_server_adv from object palette.

8. Rename AS_GRF1600_16S_AE24_F12_SLI6 router, ethernet_slip8_gtwy_adv, ip32_cloud, and ethernet_server_adv as Osaka_Router, Osaka_Firewall, Osaka_Internet, Osaka_Printer and Osaka_Workgroup_Server respectively.

9. Now go to topology menu > Rapid configuration > star configuration and click Next.

10. Select center node model as ethernet16_switch_adv, periphery node model as ethernet_wkstn_adv, and link model as 100baseT_adv.

11. Type number as 15 as we need 15 users.

12. Click ok.

13. This create 15 users connected to switch with 100 base T link, as it is connected with 100 base T link to switch, switch will become 100 base T switch.

14. Right click on each node and rename as User 1 to User 15 for 15 nodes respectively.

15. Right click on the ethernet16_switch_adv and set name as Osaka_switch.

16. Connect Osaka_Workgroup_Server, Osaka_Router to Osaka_Switch and to with 100baseT_adv link from object palette.

17. Connect Osaka_Router to Osaka_Firewall with T1 link from object palette.

18. Connect Osaka_Firewall to Osaka_Internet with T1 link from object palette.

Dileep Keshava Narayana   dileep007k@gmail.com

19. Select User 1 to User 15, Right click on any User, Select edit attributes, go to applications > Application supported profiles, click edit, Select 1 row, Select Profile names Video_Conferencing. Check mark Apply to selected objects, Click Ok again.

20. Right click on Osaka_Workgroup_Server, Select edit attributes > applications > application supported services.

21. Select 1 row and select profile name as Video_Conferencing.

22. Click on go to parent subnet from toolbar.

23. Connect WHSB_Osaka_Japan to WHSB_Tokyo_Japan with T1 link.

24. You will be asked to select node a and node b. Select node a as Tokyo_router and select node b as Osaka_Router.

25. Simulating as explained in the earlier steps and select preferences from edit. Search for network sim. Enter as stdmod in Network simulation repositories.

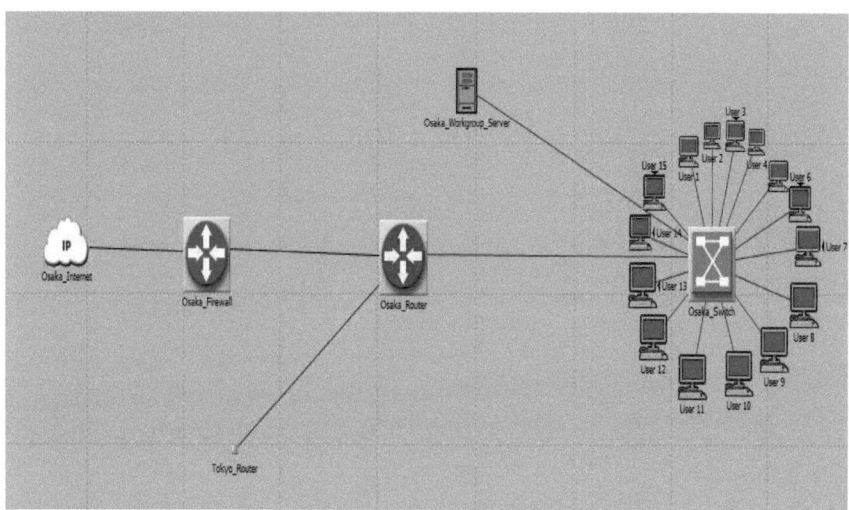

Now to investigate video conferencing follow the steps below:

Dileep Keshava Narayana
dileep007k@gmail.com

Video Conferencing

Packet Delay variation

To investigate average Packet delay variation in video conferencing, go to Results browser > Global statistics > Video Conferencing > Select Packet delay variation.

Resulting graph should resemble the following:

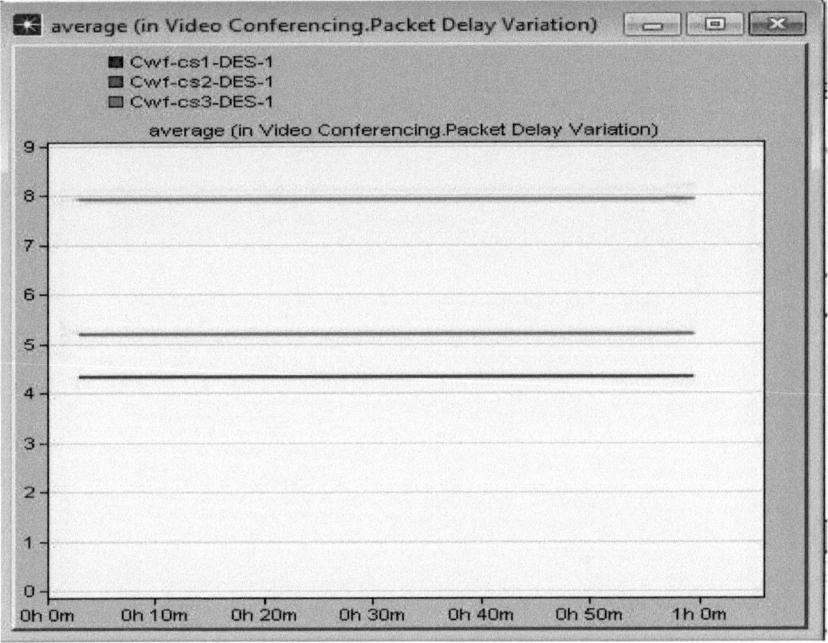

By the graph above we can analyse that, in all scenario 1, scenario 2 and scenario 3 packet delay variation is constant.

In scenario 1, Packet delay variation is low than in scenario 2.

Scenario 2 packet delay variation is lower than scenario 3.

As we have used firewall, firewall terminates ip stream in one side side of it and recreates it on other side. Even though this provides additional security in the network it might introduce some packet delay.

All scenario 1, scenario 2 and scenario 3 worked as expected.

41

Packet End-to-End Delay

Packet end to end delay is the time taken to transmit the packet from source to destination.

To investigate average Packet end to end delay in video conferencing, go to Results browser > Global statistics > Video Conferencing > Select Packet end to end delay.

Resulting graph should resemble the following:

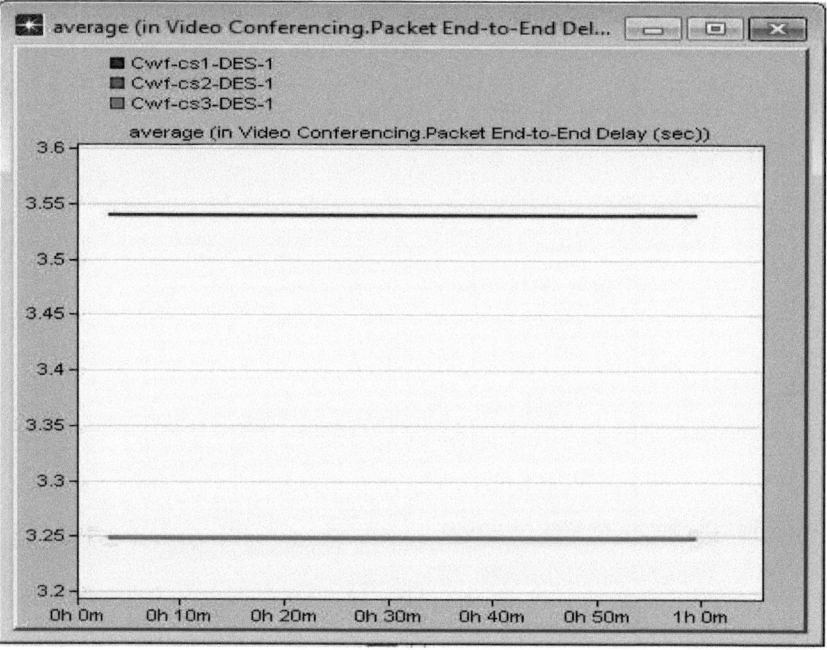

By the above graph we can analyse that the packets end to end delay in scenario 1 is more than the end to end delay in scenario 2 & scenario 3. However, packet end to end delay in all scenarios is constant.

The models worked as expected.

Dileep Keshava Narayana   dileep007k@gmail.com

Traffic received (Packets/ sec)

To investigate average Traffic received in video conferencing, go to Results browser > Global statistics > Video Conferencing > Select packets received.

Resulting graph should resemble the following:

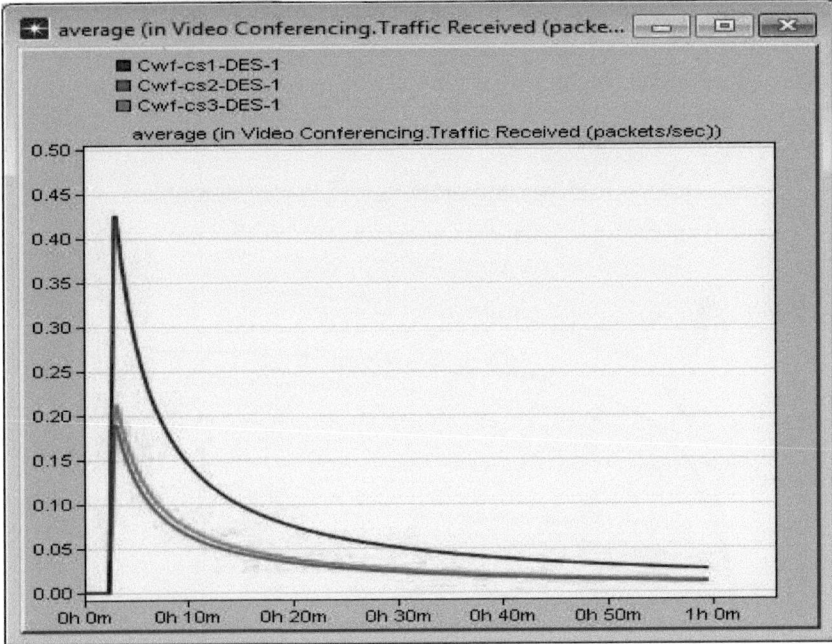

By the above graph we can analyse that the packets received in scenario 1 is more than the packets received in scenario 2 and scenario 3.

In scenario 1, the utmost packets received are 0.42 per second.

In scenario 2, the utmost packets received are 0.18 per second.

In scenario 3, the utmost packets received are 0.22 per second.

The models worked as expected.

Traffic sent (Packets/ sec)

To investigate average Traffic sent in video conferencing, go to Results browser > Global statistics > Video Conferencing > Select packets sent.

Resulting graph should resemble the following:

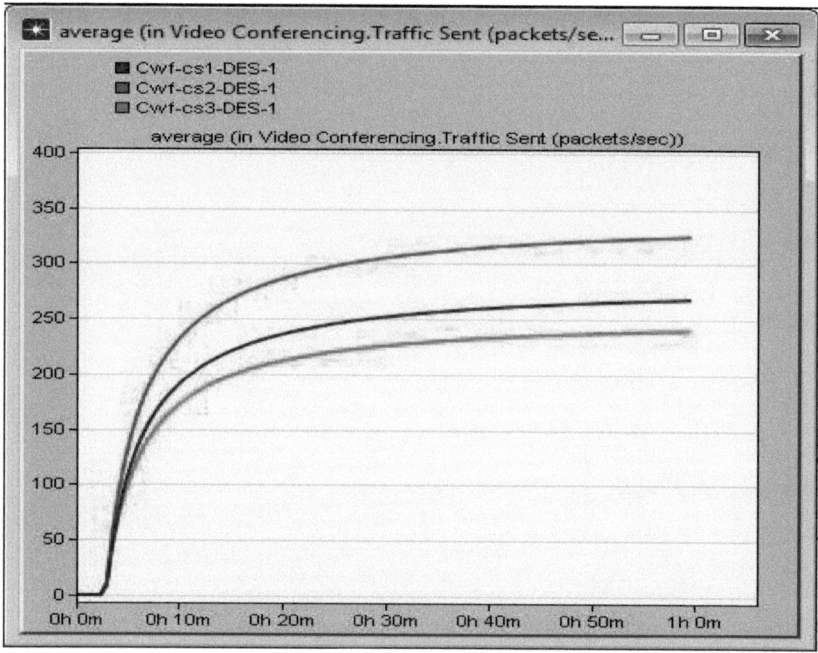

By the above graph we can analyse that in scenario 1, scenario 2 and scenario 3 the packets sent are increasing from 0 after some seconds it remains constant.

Models work as expected.

At the end, by analysing all these parameters we can tell that video conferencing application works well in the network with low packet delay and packet end to end delay.

Dileep Keshava Narayana   dileep007k@gmail.com

6. Conclusion

WHSB Organization network model has been simulated using OPNET. The utilization of the T1 link is low. We can improve the utilization of the T1 link by adding some more users, services and by replacing the 100 base T link connected to users with 1000 base T link or higher.

HTTP page response time is low. FTP average download response time is high as it uses UDP which is an unreliable protocol. So the packets can get lost in the network. So the delay is more. We can reduce the delay for the FTP by using the cloud storage devices. However, FTP load is low in the WHSB organization. So it is not wise to invest huge money for it.

The packet delay, packet end to end delay is low in general. So the voice and video conferencing application works well and it is utilized properly.

We can even increase network performance and the application performance by using ATM servers.

Dileep Keshava Narayana   dileep007k@gmail.com

Printed by Books on Demand GmbH, Norderstedt / Germany